Six One Acts

Brett C Leonard

BROADWAY PLAY PUBLISHING INC
New York
BroadwayPlayPub.com

First printing: November 2019
I S B N: 978-0-88145-548-9

Book design: Marie Donovan
Page make-up: Adobe InDesign
Typeface: Palatino

CONTENTS

NOTE ON MUSIC

For performance of copyrighted songs, arrangements
or recordings referenced in this play, permission
of the copyright owner(s) must be obtained. Other
songs, arrangements or recordings may be substituted
provided permission from the copyright owner(s) of
such songs, arrangements or recordings is obtained
or songs, arrangements or recordings in the public
domain may be substituted.

For Elizabeth
For everything
For always

SNAPSHOT

SNAPSHOT was originally performed in 2011 at the Annual Summer Intensive of LAByrinth Theater Company (Artistic Directors, Stephen Adly Guirgis, Mimi O'Donnell, & Yul Vázquez; Managing Director, Danny Feldman). The cast and creative contributor were:

SAMUEL... Gregg Henry
FRANKIE...Ed Vassallo
LADY ABIGAIL ....Maggie Flanigan
DASHIELL...Trevor Long
JIMMYLARK ....Max Casella
BERRIAN..Kevin Geer

Director .... Brett C Leonard

SNAPSHOT was subsequently presented in New York City as part of LAByrinth Theater Company's Barn Series 2011. The cast and creative contributor were:

SAMUEL.. Gregg Henry
FRANKIE.. David Wilson Barnes
LADY ABIGAIL...Maggie Burke
DASHIELL...Trevor Long
JIMMYLARK .... Max Casella
BERRIAN..Kevin Geer

Director ....Mimi O'Donnell

SNAPSHOT was produced by Collaboraction Theater Company (Artistic Director, Anthony Moseley) in Chicago in 2012. The cast and creative contributor were:

SAMUEL..Karl Potthoff
FRANKIE... Daniel McEvilly
LADY ABIGAIL .... Morgan McCabe
DASHIELL...Ryan Dolan
JIMMYLARK ....Chris Meister
BERRIAN...Foster Williams

Director .... Anthony Moseley

CHARACTERS & SETTING

SAMUEL, *60s*
FRANKIE, *30s*
LADY ABIGAIL, *50s-60*
DASHIELL, *30s*
BERRIAN, *50s*
JIMMYLARK, *30s*

Setting: A town in America

A cinderblock basement. A master suite. A bar. A kitchen/ dining room.

for the lives and memories of
Ed Vassallo and Kevin Geer

Scene 1

(A nondescript room. Cinder block walls.)

(SAMUEL, 60s, is tied to a chair. His mouth is taped and gagged. FRANKIE, 30s, is on his feet.)

FRANKIE: A man walks into a bar with his two young sons, children. The bartender asks, "what would you like to drink?" The man pulls out a gun and shoots the bartender in the face. The man pours himself a drink, a low-grade tequila. None of the customers or his children say a word. The man finishes his drink and leaves what he considers to be a fair gratuity. The next day he walks into another bar, once again with his two sons. The bartender says "may I help you?" The man shoots him in the neck. No one seems to object, not audibly. The man pours himself a drink—a draft this time. "Beamish Irish Stout." He enjoyed it so much he had himself a second one before once again leaving a more than acceptable gratuity. On the following day he visits a third bar with similar results—a greeting, a gunshot, a drink—gin and tonic this time. The man drank free for three days straight. No one spoke to him, no one approached, no one called the police. He liked that. He was amongst fellow drinkers. Drunks. The good kind. The ones didn't flap their lips and get stupid. Flappity-flappity. *(Beat)* On a different day, or perhaps it was one of the three aforementioned, it's not the point… this same man…he walks his dog. A few nights earlier his dog wouldn't stop barking, kept the man awake. This was a man who cherished his sleep.

He got cranky when he went without, his eyes would get puffy. Black. Heavy bags. This was a vain man. He didn't like dark circles under his eyes. So he took a knife, not unlike this one… *(Takes out a knife)* …and went out to the yard. He cut his dog's tongue out. No more barking. No more noise. The man had a mostly pleasant night sleep, but for the occasional muffled whimpers of his tongueless dog. The following day the man walked the dog. The dog's name was Purlie. She was of pure breeding from a long line of show dogs. Golden Retrievers. Cocky dogs. Think they're better than other dogs. *(Beat)* Purlie sees an old woman, an elderly woman in a flower-print dress. She gets her purse snatched by a fellow small in stature but fast with his hands and faster on his feet. Purlie has no tongue, she cannot bark. But she could have run after the small statured man and taken him to the ground. She could have bitten into his neck and let him bleed out. But she did not. Neither did her owner. He did nothing. *(Beat)* Many things can be accomplished without a tongue. Singing can be difficult but roller blading is not. One need not a tongue to roller blade in the park. One need not a tongue to run a marathon. Or to bite a man who runs one. To attack. To stand one's ground. One need not a tongue to cut out the tongue of another. One need not a tongue to make his presence known in the world. Presence is more important than noise. Endless chatter of the rah-rah blah-blah variety. *(Beat)* There is too much noise. It never goes away. It eats at you from the outside-in, from the inside-out. It never leaves you alone, the blah blah. The rah-rah-rah.

(FRANKIE quickly grabs SAMUEL's head, rips off the tape, pulls the cloth out of his mouth, pulls out his tongue and slices it. He doesn't cut it out, he just slices. SAMUEL does his best to try to speak.)

SAMUEL: What are you…

(FRANKIE *slices* SAMUEL's *tongue once again.*)

SAMUEL: —aggh, why are you?—

(FRANKIE *slices again.*)

SAMUEL: —Aggh—

(*And slices again.* FRANKIE *quickly stuffs the cloth back in* SAMUEL's *mouth, tapes his mouth shut, then runs off, slamming the door with the eight dead bolts behind him.*)

(*We hear him lock the eight dead-bolts from outside the door as* SAMUEL *struggles, blood appears on the tape. He tries to hop across the room, toward the door. He falls, spills onto the ground. He reaches out, tries to talk...nothing comes.*)

Scene 2

(*A fancy bedroom. A four-post bed. Antique furniture. A well-dressed woman,* LADY ABIGAIL, *50s-60s, teaches a well-dressed young man,* DASHIELL, *30s, how to dance as they listen to Mozart's Violin Concerto #3 in G. [Suggested: Takako Nishizaki's recording]*).

(*A man in a tuxedo, a butler—*BERRIAN, *50s—stands and watches, silently and perfectly still.*)

LADY ABIGAIL: Feet... Feet... Feet... Feet... Feet... Foot... Right... Foot... Right... Right... Right... Right... Right... Right... Right... Foot... Right... Right... Left... Good... Two... Three... Four... Good... Right... Right... Right... Good... Feet... Right... Right... Right... Right... Left... Two... Three... Four... Good.

(DASHIELL *and* LADY ABIGAIL *stop dancing. She kisses him on the mouth.*)

LADY ABIGAIL: Good.

(LADY ABIGAIL *moves to the record player. She stands above it, listens to the music, her eyes staring at the record going round and round.* DASHIELL *watches her from the middle of the room.)*

*(*LADY ABIGAIL *turns and looks at* DASHIELL.*)*

LADY ABIGAIL: You may leave.

*(*DASHIELL *nods. He leaves.)*

*(*LADY ABIGAIL *listens to the music.)*

(She closes her eyes.)

(She begins to waltz…alone.)

*(*BERRIAN *watches.)*

(Teddy Thompson's One of These Days *begins—drowning out Mozart's* Concerto #3*—as the lights fade on* LADY ABIGAIL *and rise on…)*

Scene 3

(A Bar. One of These Days *blasts too loud.)*

*(*FRANKIE *is sitting at the bar. Drinking. Shots. Beers. Paying zero attention to* JIMMYLARK, *30s, drunk, happy, enthusiastic, lots of energy, talking at the top of his lungs at a million miles an hour.)*

JIMMYLARK: That's the thing about all of 'em! Women! People! Men! People! Everybody gotta have somebody to make everybody feel like they ain't a nobody who ain't better than somebody! Me, you, the pygmies in Kalamazoo, friends, neighbors, the you-know-who'ers—everyone! This chick says "Jimmylark, Jimmylark, a lark like a bird"—tits out to here—"like a parakeet", she says—a lark an' a parakeet, wha' do I say? Tits out to here. "Can I buy you a drink?", I say, "Jimmylark would like to buy you a drink and sing like a songbird jailbird parakeet dove as he eats your ass and plays with your disproportionately large titties." Out to here, Frankie. Jimmylark teases, Big

Tits pleases. Jimmylark sings, when he pisses it stings.
(Checks his watch) Where is this prick? *(Pulls out a gun)*
Bang bang he's dead but I'm alive. Alive and kickin'.
(He kicks the air.) Alive an' dancin'! *(Dances)* I wanna
dance, you wanna dance? I like to dance. It's a part
of who I am. Dancing! I like dancing and I like my
gun. Big parts of who I am. You like to drink and play
golf—I like to dance. And my gun! I really really really
really really really like my gun! *(Dances for a while, then)*
It's freeing! Dancing! You learn a lot about yourself
when you forget who you are! The more you get LOST,
the more you get FOUND! Not like a fuckin, you
know, found like a fuckin—not like found like found
like fuckin' Jesus and shit, just... you know, you dance,
you get lost, you get found. I'm not gonna make more
of it than what needs to be made. *(Dances)* NINETY-
EIGHT PERCENT WATER, HA! All of us. *(Dances,
checks watch)* Where the fuck is this prick? So this
Mount Everest of mammaries, this chick, swear to all
three fuckin' Wisemen and their gifts a' bullshit—even
though she thinks she's better than me and insulted
me and my technique and stamina and my size, and
even though she gave me this burn in my urethra that
refuses to go away...I loved her, Frankie. I fuckin'
loved her. Like a human being loves another human
being. She was a human being, I am a human being.
She was a human person and human persons gotta
find ways to feel better about themselves by thinkin'
worse about others and by inflicting a degree of pain
and suffering they deem appropriate and necessary to
assure their own survival and modicum of self-esteem.
We all do, Frankie, every one of us—me, you, the
monkeys of Kalamazoo. We all gotta shit on someone,
Frankie. Shit on or be shat upon. At least she chose me!
She chose me, Frankie, and I chose her. And I loved her
very much. For thirty-five minutes she was the only
thing I ever loved. It was a beautiful night an' love at

first sight. *(Checks watch)* **Where the fuck is this prick?** *(He shoots the ceiling four times. Blackout/silence)*

Scene 4

(Teddy Thompson's Turning the Gun on Myself *rises softly as lights rise slowly on the cinder block room.)*

*(*SAMUEL *is still on the ground, dried blood on his chin and neck. Unconscious or asleep. Eyes closed.)*

*(The dead-bolts on the door begin to unlock one at a time. After all eight are unlocked…*DASHIELL *enters. Dressed as we saw him in his bedroom waltz.)*

(He looks at SAMUEL *on the ground. He stares.* SAMUEL's *eyes remain closed.* DASHIELL *slowly approaches. He looks around—no one, nothing. Just a windowless room, a bucket in a corner, a roll of toilet paper, a wooden stool, stacks and stacks of books.)*

(He looks at his watch and checks his pulse in his neck. Ten seconds.)

(He then approaches, gets closer, hesitates. Leans down)

*(*SAMUEL *suddenly opens his eyes, lifts his head.)*

*(*DASHIELL *quickly punches him in the face. Blackout/ silence)*

Scene 5

*(*LADY ABIGAIL's *kitchen.* LADY ABIGAIL, FRANKIE, JIMMYLARK.)*

*(*BERRIAN *tends to the meal around the table with the chandelier dangling overhead. Tea. Wine. Champagne. Boiled eggs. Scones. Crackers. Cheese. Finger sandwiches. Soup. Shrimp cocktails. Chocolate fondue. Ice cream. Sushi. Cotton candy, both pink and blue)*

(LADY ABIGAIL *eats pink cotton candy.* JIMMYLARK *eats blue. And lots of other food too.*)

(FRANKIE *drinks wine. Lots of wine. Then champagne. Then wine again. He has an incredibly high tolerance. Or rather, it's hard for others to tell when he's drunk. But he always knows. Except when he's in a blackout, which he may be in now. Another reason why he didn't have* JIMMYLARK *wait in the car…he may need someone to tell him what happened and what was said at a later time when he's sober and knows for a fact he'll remember it.*)

JIMMYLARK: The yellowtail sushi with the blue cotton candy is particularly delightful, Lady Abigail. It's my second favorite to the boiled eggs dipped in chocolate fondue.

LADY ABIGAIL: Abigail.

JIMMYLARK: Yes.

LADY ABIGAIL: Just…Abigail. Not "Lady" Abigail.

JIMMYLARK: Oh.

LADY ABIGAIL: Just Abigail.

JIMMYLARK: Okay.

LADY ABIGAIL: Go on. It's okay.

JIMMYLARK: Abigail.

LADY ABIGAIL: Yes. Say it again.

JIMMYLARK: Abigail.

LADY ABIGAIL: Good.

JIMMYLARK: Hey there…Abigail. Hello there. What's shakin', Abigail? Too much?

LADY ABIGAIL: No.

(LADY ABIGAIL *eats her pink cotton candy and looks at* FRANKIE, *who doesn't look at her. She looks back at* JIMMYLARK.)

LADY ABIGAIL: Even…Abby, if you like.

JIMMYLARK: Abby.

LADY ABIGAIL: If you prefer.

JIMMYLARK: I don't know. I like 'em both.

(JIMMYLARK *looks at* FRANKIE, *who doesn't look at him.*)

JIMMYLARK: Wha'do you think? Abby or Abigail?

(No response)

JIMMYLARK: You think Abby or Abigail?

(No response)

JIMMYLARK: *(To* LADY ABIGAIL*)* Lemme think about it.

LADY ABIGAIL: Do you dance?

JIMMYLARK: …What?

LADY ABIGAIL: Dance? Do you dance?

JIMMYLARK: I'm a dancer! It's a part of who I am! It is a major part of who I am!

LADY ABIGAIL: Berrian?

(BERRIAN *goes to the turntable. He places the needle on the record.*)

(*Mozart's* Violin Concerto #3 in G *begins to play.*)

(LADY ABIGAIL *rises…dances alone.* FRANKIE *pours himself another glass of red wine, pays no attention to* LADY ABIGAIL's *dancing.* JIMMYLARK *watches* FRANKIE *drink. Then watches* LADY ABIGAIL *waltzing alone, her eyes shut.*)

(BERRIAN *watches too.*)

(JIMMYLARK *stands. He moves slowly, a slight dance.*)

(LADY ABIGAIL *opens her eyes, stops dancing. She sees* JIMMYLARK *dancing. He stops. They look at each other—her with the pink cotton candy in her hand, him with the blue.*)

(*She curtsies from across the room. He bows.*)

(FRANKIE *drinks.*)

(BERRIAN *watches.*)

(LADY ABIGAIL *dances.* JIMMYLARK *dances. Ten feet between them. They stare at each other as they continue. They approach one another. They eat from each other's cotton candy.*)

(LADY ABIGAIL *takes both cotton candies and throws them over her shoulder…*BERRIAN *retrieves them. He stands watching—blue cotton candy in one hand, pink in the other.*)

(LADY ABIGAIL *and* JIMMYLARK *dance.* FRANKIE *pours another drink.*)

(LADY ABIGAIL *and* JIMMYLARK *begin to kiss. Softly. Slowly. They stop.*)

(LADY ABIGAIL *moves for the exit.*)

(BERRIAN *turns off the music.*)

(BERRIAN *opens the door for* LADY ABIGAIL, *follows her out.*)

(JIMMYLARK *looks at* FRANKIE.)

JIMMYLARK: Dude?

(FRANKIE *pours himself a glass of wine, no eye contact.*)

JIMMYLARK: Dude?

(*No response*)

JIMMYLARK: Dude? (*He approaches.*) Dude, your mom just kissed me.

FRANKIE: YOU DANCE LIKE A FAGGOT, JIMMY! YOU DANCE LIKE A LITTLE GIRL!

(FRANKIE *grabs a candlestick holder, leaps to his feet, bends* JIMMYLARK *over the table, pulls at* JIMMYLARK'S *pants and tries to shove the candlestick holder up his ass…as:*)

(*Overlapping:*)

FRANKIE: You wanna get fucked? Huh? I'll fuck you, Jimmy—I WILL FUCK YOU!

JIMMYLARK: *(Overlapping)* Hey, hey, stop it—stop! Stop!

(FRANKIE *stops, tosses aside the candlestick holder.* JIMMYLARK *pulls up his pants.)*

JIMMYLARK: Fuck'samatter with you?

FRANKIE: Fuck'samatter with you?

(FRANKIE *sits, sips wine. Long pause)*

JIMMYLARK: You alright? *(Beat)* Hey. *(Beat)* You alright? *(Beat)* Frankie? *(Beat)* Hey. *(Beat)* I was fuckin' around.

(FRANKIE *drinks, says nothing.* JIMMYLARK *goes to the table, sits. He pours himself a glass of wine.)*

(Silence. They drink.)

(JIMMYLARK *checks his watch.)*

JIMMYLARK: Where is this prick? He was supposed to meet us at the bar.

FRANKIE: We're not at the bar.

JIMMYLARK: But that's where he was supposed to meet us.

FRANKIE: Well, he didn't.

JIMMYLARK: Maybe he did but we left before he got there.

FRANKIE: If ya hadn't a gotten stupid and started shootin' the place up—

JIMMYLARK: —I'm not stupid—

FRANKIE: —maybe we woulda waited longer—

JIMMYLARK: —I shot the roof—

FRANKIE: —and he woulda shown up—

JIMMYLARK: —the ceiling—

FRANKIE: —before we had to get outta there—

JIMMYLARK: —not the place—

FRANKIE: —before the fuckin' cops came.

JIMMYLARK: It was the ceiling I shot, Frank. The ceiling ain't the place. You said the place. If I hadn't a started shootin' up the place.

(Pause. They drink. JIMMYLARK checks his watch.)

JIMMYLARK: It wasn't the place, Frank. It was the ceiling.

(FRANKIE drinks, ignores JIMMYLARK.)

JIMMYLARK: I wanna dance, man. Shit like this? Tension? Nerves? When I feel anxiety creep, I wanna dance. *(Rocks shoulders a little)* Work it out. Move it around. From the brain to the shoulders. Shoulders to the arms. *(Eyes closed)* Down the body. Get the knees movin'. Toes. The pelvis. Gyrate in little circles. Thrust, mm. Thrust, yeah. Slow and subtle. Highly sexual. Hear it. Feel it. I'm feelin' it, baby—you feelin' it? Oh yeah. Hello dance, goodbye stress.

FRANKIE: SHUT THE FUCK UP, WOULD YOU SHUT THE FUCK UP, WOULD YOU SHUT THE FUCK UP, WOULD YOU SHUT THE FUCK UP, SHUT THE FUCK UP!!!

(From offstage—)

LADY ABIGAIL: STOP STOP STOP STOP STOP!!!!!!!!!

(FRANKIE stops yelling. JIMMYLARK stops talking, moving. They look in the direction of LADY ABIGAIL's voice.)

(Silence)

Scene 6

(The cinder block room)

*(*DASHIELL *sits in a corner, eating a baguette. Staring at* SAMUEL, *whose eyes are open. They stare at each other.)*

*(*DASHIELL *checks his watch, checks his pulse in his neck. Ten seconds.)*

(He approaches, crawling. Stops. Sits up on his knees. Looks at SAMUEL. SAMUEL *looks at him.)*

(Silence. Then…)

DASHIELL: Hello. *(Beat)* Samuel. *(Beat)* Hello.

*(*SAMUEL *doesn't respond.* DASHIELL *gets more comfortable, crosses his legs, sitting on the ground. Stares at* SAMUEL. *Eats his baguette, looking at* SAMUEL, SAMUEL *looking at him.)*

DASHIELL: Everyone remembers things different. Maybe forgetting isn't so bad. Maybe forgetting is…maybe it's actually best. The good and the bad. Maybe…maybe forgetting is what we're supposed to do. Or maybe it's our, it's our *reward*…y'know? Like if we've done more bad than good or…had more bad than good done *to us*…but we still did a lotta good but people wanna remind us and remember the bad shit, y'know? Maybe it's our reward. Forgetting. A clean slate. To the beginning. Everybody just…everybody just… gets a second chance. No. Not chance, just… Everybody gets nothing. Nothing…nothing to remember…nothing to forget. Maybe better. Y'know? Maybe that's best. *(Long pause. He eats his baguette.)* Your hands hurt? Mm? Your hands? Your wrists?

*(*SAMUEL *has no response, simply continues to stare.)*

DASHIELL: What about your mouth? What he do to you? Why'd he do that? *(Beat)* Want me to look? *(Beat)* Want me to look? Mm? *(Beat)* Want me to take a look?

(No response)

DASHIELL: Want me to read a book? Huh? I could read you a book…if you want? You like books, right? Spy novels? Tom Clancy. Let me see who we got. *(He checks the stacks of books, throwing one after another after another after another over his shoulder as he sorts through the stack.)* A, A, A, A, B, B, B, B. C… Here we go—C… Camus. Camus. Camus. Camus. Celine. Celine. Celine. Calvino. Chekhov. Chekhov. Camus. Chekhov. Conrad. Conrad. Chaucer. Cleland. Coleridge. Congreve. Congreve. Cooper. Crane. Conrad. Camus. Camus. Conrad. Chekhov. Calvino. Calvino. Celine. Camus. Conrad. Camus. Camus. Camus. *(Looks to* SAMUEL*)* No Tom Clancy. Who else writes spy novels? *(Scans the books)* Spy novels. Books of intrigue? Page-turners-you-can't-put-down? Who else? Who else? *(Looks at* SAMUEL*)* Who else?

*(*SAMUEL *gestures with his head toward a bag in the corner.* DASHIELL *goes to it. He opens it. He takes out an old paperback book.)*

(He looks at his father.)

(Pause)

Scene 7

(The bar)

(Ornette Coleman's "Eventually" blasts as FRANKIE *drinks and* JIMMYLARK *dances.)*

JIMMYLARK: I think we oughtta go soon! I think we should wrap it up and head out soon! I think we should either find him or kill him! Or maybe he's already dead! We gotta forget him and check on Samuel! Dashiell's a damaged man, Frankie! A disturbed child of epic proportions! A giant of an infant

who cannot be depended upon! We must do what we
need to do with him or without him! This is your thing,
not mine, I'm along for the ride and the company and
I'm not complaining, I just think we're makin' too
many pit stops along the way. I know you wanna do
things the way you wanna do 'em, but sometimes our
wants and our gets are extremely fuckin' divided! I
think this is one of those times, Frankie! I think we go
to where we gotta go to do the thing you want done
with or without fuckin' you-know-who! It's your thing,
Frankie! I'm not complaining! I'm merely suggesting!
I'm suggesting we do things different than we planned!
Differently. Frankie! Frankie! Things never go according
to fucking plan!

(JIMMYLARK *dances,* FRANKIE *drinks.*)

Scene 8

(DASHIELL *reads Dashiell Hammett's* The Thin Man.
SAMUEL *stares at him.*)

DASHIELL: Blah-blah-blah. Blah-blah-blah. Blah-blah.
Blah-blah-blah-blah-blah-blah. Blah. "The End." (*He
closes the book, moved. He enjoyed it. He stares at it.*) He's
a genius. A genius genius. A double genius. I can't
believe I'm named after him. What a gift. What a
special gift. Hammett. Dashiell Hammett. A genius,
genius. My namesake. (*To* SAMUEL) My namesake.
(*Sincerely*) Thank you.

(DASHIELL *looks at* SAMUEL. *Smiles.* SAMUEL *stares, no
smile.* SAMUEL *motions towards the bucket.*)

DASHIELL: What? You need to drop one? Huh? (*Beat*)
Shit or piss? (*Beat*) Number one or number two? (*Beat*)
One or two? (*Beat*) Yellow or brown? (*Beat*) Urine or
feces? (*Beat*) Lemonade or chocolate bar?

(SAMUEL *pees his pants.* DASHIELL *runs to help.*)

DASHIELL: Oh no, no. Sorry, no, I'm... *(He takes off his shirt, starts dabbing it on* SAMUEL's *crotch.)* Here, here. There ya go, sop it right up. Be all dry in a minute. All dry. No one will notice, no one will care. *(He stops. He speaks almost to himself:)* No one will notice. No one will care. *(Pause. Then...he continues to dry* SAMUEL's *pants with his shirt.)* Almost dry already. Good as new. Good as new.

*(*DASHIELL *moves away.* SAMUEL's *pants are soaked with urine. Samuel looks down at his wet pants.)*

DASHIELL: I'm sorry. I'm sorry. *(He looks at his watch, checks his pulse in his neck. 10 seconds)* I'm so sorry.

*(*SAMUEL *stares at him.)*

Scene 9

(The bar)

(R L Burnside's Someday Baby *blasts.* FRANKIE *drinks and drinks and drinks.* JIMMYLARK *dances and dances and dances—waving his gun in the air.)*

*(Eventually...*FRANKIE *takes out his own gun. He slowly lets the music begin to affect him. He stands. He moves a little. Then a little more)*

(He dances.)

(He readies himself for what needs to get done.)

(They both dance, guns waving in the air.)

(Silence/black)

Scene 10

(In darkness…we hear the eight deadbolt locks being unlocked. Click. Click. Click. Click…)

(As the lights slowly rise on…the cinder block room.)

(Nobody's in it. Just the bucket, stool, books thrown all over the room.)

(FRANKIE and JIMMYLARK enter. Burnside's "Someday Baby" begins once again. Blasts)

(FRANKIE and JIMMYLARK look around the room. FRANKIE picks up a few books, drops them on the floor.)

(They go to the chair. The ropes have all been untied.)

(They look at the seat—it's wet.)

(FRANKIE touches it. He smells his fingers.)

(He looks around.)

(He looks down. He sees a book, one book, off to the side, all alone.)

*(He picks it up—*The Thin Man* by Dashiell Hammett. He opens it. He reads. He closes it.)*

(FRANKIE exits. JIMMYLARK follows.)

Scene 11

(DASHIELL, FRANKIE, JIMMYLARK and LADY ABIGAIL sit around a table in LADY ABIGAIL's home.)

(BERRIAN serves dessert, clears plates.)

(SAMUEL enters, dragging a large black plastic trash bag. Golf club handles stick out of the top. As does a plastic vacuum attachment, the kind used to vacuum ceilings.)

(He has changed his pants, he wears a nice shirt and a tie that reads "I'm Too Sexy For My Tie". He looks shorter standing up than he did in the chair. He looks older. His

sliced tongue makes him sound like he's suffered a major stroke. In fact, he has. Or has he?)

SAMUEL: I'm glad you're all here. It's been a long time.

FRANKIE: It hasn't been that long.

DASHIELL: *(To* FRANKIE*)* Shut up.

FRANKIE: It hasn't been a long time.

SAMUEL: I know how much you love your hobby, Frankie.

FRANKIE: It's not a hobby.

DASHIELL: Shut up.

SAMUEL: It's been a long time.

FRANKIE: *(To* SAMUEL*)* What are you doing?

DASHIELL: Would you shut up?

*(*SAMUEL *struggles with the duct tape he's used to wrap around the trash bag.)*

SAMUEL: I can't seem to get this to… It's sticking…

JIMMYLARK: Want some help, Mister Reynolds?

SAMUEL: It's more difficult than—

JIMMYLARK: —Let me help.

SAMUEL: I DON'T NEED HELP! *(Then quietly)* I don't need help. *(He tries to undo the duct tape once again.)* I spent three hours putting this together for you, Frankie.

FRANKIE: It's Frank.

SAMUEL: It shouldn't take as long to take apart.

*(*FRANKIE *whips out his knife and aggressively pulls the bag out of* SAMUEL*'s hand, he cuts the tape with the knife as:)*

FRANKIE: Ya don't need help?!—

DASHIELL: —Hey—

FRANKIE: —Ya don't need help, ya fuckin' phony—

DASHIELL: —You're giving him a stroke!—

FRANKIE: —You fuckin' fraud—

DASHIELL: —Leave him alone—

FRANKIE: —I'm not doing anything!—

JIMMYLARK: —Let it alone, Frank—

FRANKIE: —I'm tryin' to help—

SAMUEL: —I DON'T WANT HELP!—

DASHIELL: —What the fuck're you doing?—

JIMMYLARK: Leave'm alone, Frank.

(FRANKIE *stops with the trash bag filled with golf clubs, turns his knife on* JIMMYLARK.)

FRANKIE: You got somewhere to go, go! Go to your own fuckin' family!

(FRANKIE *continues to cut the duct tape from the trash bag.*)

(LADY ABIGAIL *begins to sing the chorus of Alison Kraus's* When You Say Nothing At All.)

LADY ABIGAIL: —"The smile on your face lets me know that you need me"—

FRANKIE: (*To* SAMUEL) —ya fuckin' liar!—

DASHIELL: (*Checking his pulse*) —fuck're you doing?

LADY ABIGAIL: —"There's a truth in your eyes saying you'll never leave me"—

SAMUEL: (*To* LADY ABIGAIL) What'd I do?

DASHIELL: (*To* FRANKIE) Leave'm alone!

LADY ABIGAIL: —"The touch of your hand says you'll catch me if ever I fall"—

SAMUEL: (*To* LADY ABIGAIL) —What I do?—

DASHIELL: —Frankie, stop—

FRANKIE: You're not *allowed* to forget!

JIMMYLARK: C'mon, Frank.

FRANKIE: *(To* SAMUEL*)* —You want your fuckin' trash bag, you want your center of attention, you want your fuckin' spotlight!—

DASHIELL: Goddamnit!

SAMUEL: *(To* LADY ABIGAIL*)* What I do?

LADY ABIGAIL: —"You say it best when you say nothing at all"—

DASHIELL: *(To* FRANKIE*)* —STOP IT!—

FRANKIE: *(To* SAMUEL*)* —Take it!

*(*FRANKIE *pushes the now open bag toward* SAMUEL...*just as Dashiell lunges for* FRANKIE. FRANKIE *turns, the knife in his hand, it slices* DASHIELL*'s arm, who grabs it, bleeding, scoots across the floor on his ass, away from* FRANKIE.*)*

DASHIELL: Sonuvabitch! You cut me.

FRANKIE: It was an accident.

DASHIELL: You sliced my arm.

FRANKIE: Jesus Christ, you're dramatic.

DASHIELL: I'm bleeding.

FRANKIE: You shouldn'ta lunged.

DASHIELL: What?

FRANKIE: You lunged.

DASHIELL: I was trying to protect him.

FRANKIE: You lunged.

DASHIELL: I was trying to protect him.

JIMMYLARK: *(To* LADY ABIGAIL*)* You have a lovely voice.

LADY ABIGAIL: I haven't sung in a long time.

SAMUEL: *(To* FRANKIE, *taking out a golf putter)* When you first started putting, you had difficulty with the weight of the club head. It was this style of putter, if not this precise putter. Which it may be, I'm not sure. So I worked on adding weight to your new putter, when you were just a boy, if you recall. I do.

FRANKIE: Of course you do.

(SAMUEL *pulls out a second club, this one has batteries duct-taped to the head of the club.)*

SAMUEL: And the weight problem had been solved. But you believed it was too short. You had grown, had a… you had a… *(He looks to* LADY ABIGAIL *for help.)*

DASHIELL: Growth spurt.

SAMUEL: What?

DASHIELL: He had a growth spurt, Dad.

FRANKIE: This is such horseshit.

SAMUEL: Is everything okay?

FRANKIE: I'm having the time of my life.

SAMUEL: That's great, son.

FRANKIE: It was a joke.

DASHIELL: *(Still checking his pulse)* Leave him alone.

FRANKIE: Fuck you.

LADY ABIGAIL: We said we weren't going to do this.

SAMUEL: The next club I made for you addressed your height concerns. You had such trouble with the short clubs—

FRANKIE: —I didn't have such trouble—

LADY ABIGAIL: —We were all going to get along—

DASHIELL: —I love you, Mom—

SAMUEL: —So I built you something like this—

FRANKIE: —I didn't have trouble—

(SAMUEL *pulls out a normal height golf putter with a vacuum extension duct taped to the club handle, adding two feet to the length. He stands as he demonstrates.*)

SAMUEL: —To put the club handle against your chest, to stabilize it, nice easy swing…like this.

LADY ABIGAIL: We're family.

DASHIELL: I love you, Mom.

SAMUEL: *(To* FRANKIE*)* Would you like to try it?

FRANKIE: No.

SAMUEL: I made it for you.

FRANKIE: I don't wanna.

SAMUEL: I have more in the bag. Different kinds.

FRANKIE: I said no.

SAMUEL: Lighter. Heavier.

DASHIELL: I'll try.

SAMUEL: *(To* FRANKIE*)* I made it for you.

DASHIELL: Here, dad, I'll try.

FRANKIE: He doesn't want you to try, he wants me to try. If you had shown up to the fuckin' bar we wouldn't have this problem.

DASHIELL: I went to the *place*!

FRANKIE: We said the *bar*, then the place!

DASHIELL: Look at him! Look at him!

FRANKIE: *(Into* SAMUEL'*s eyes)* Hello Samuel, Hello Daddy, how are you, it's a pleasure to see you again! I always enjoy your company SO MUCH, DADDY!

DASHIELL: Ignore him, Pop.

FRANKIE: Ignore me, Pop—ignore me—you know how to do that, right? *(He grabs* SAMUEL's *face:)* Look at me! Look at me!

*(*LADY ABIGAIL *snaps. It is a side of her we haven't seen, a side of her she has tucked away for a long, long time. During this,* FRANKIE *releases* SAMUEL's *face.)*

LADY ABIGAIL: Stop it! Stop! We were not going to do this, we were NOT going to do this, we were NOT going to do this! We weren't going to talk about each other or ourselves, or our lives, or our pasts, or our futures, or our presents. Or politics or religion or the weather. Or about television or movies or music. We are not to speak of anything that could possibly have a differing opinion!

*(*SAMUEL *has already taken his seat.* FRANKIE *sits.)*

(Beat. LADY ABIGAIL *continues:)*

LADY ABIGAIL: We will count our blessings. We will pass the rolls and butter and carrots and broccoli souffle around the table. I love each and every one of you and am very proud of you. I'm happy you're doing so well, Frankie. I'm proud of you, Dashiell, for growing into a…healthy, handsome young man. I've enjoyed getting to know *you*, Jimmylark. You have soft and sensitive hands. Berrian, my most trusted and loyal friend. You are trusted and loyal. And Samuel. Yes. Most of all…Samuel. Forty-three years. Forty-three. Yes. Forty-three.

*(*FRANKIE *and* SAMUEL *are at the table.* FRANKIE *pours* SAMUEL *a glass of red wine. He pours a glass for himself.)*

*(*LADY ABIGAIL *walks to the record player. She puts the needle down—Mozart's* Violin Concerto #3 *begins to play, softly.)*

*(*DASHIELL *cries in a corner, rocking back and forth, knees tucked into his chest.)*

FRANKIE: You wanna hear a story, Pop?

SAMUEL: A story?

FRANKIE: It's a good story. It's a father-son story.

SAMUEL: I like stories.

FRANKIE: Yeah. This is uh...a father-son story...two sons...they walk into a bar. The father and two sons. The oldest one's six. The younger just turned three. The father puts the younger one on the bar. He puts the older son—the six-year-old—on a stool beside him. The father stays on his feet. A family field trip. "Ssshh... Don't tell your mother." The bartender asks "what would you like to drink"? The father says "I'd like a Beamish Irish Stout". Have you heard this one, Pop? Sound familiar?

SAMUEL: Who?

FRANKIE: This story, Pop? Do you know this story?

SAMUEL: Do I know you?

DASHIELL: *(Re: his pulse)* It's a hundred and thirty. I can't get it below a hundred and thirty.

FRANKIE: You don't know me?

SAMUEL: Of course I know you.

FRANKIE: Who am I?

SAMUEL: You work here. You take care of me.

FRANKIE: I take care of you?

DASHIELL: It's up to a hundred and forty.

FRANKIE: I'm your nurse?

SAMUEL: You're my friend.

DASHIELL: I can't get it below a hundred and forty.

(LADY ABIGAIL stands, offers a hand to JIMMYLARK. JIMMYLARK rises.)

FRANKIE: So, the father orders a Beamish Irish Stout. The bartender delivers the drink.

DASHIELL: A hundred and fifty. It's getting worse.

(JIMMYLARK *and* LADY ABIGAIL *begin to dance.*)

(BERRIAN *continues to watch.*)

FRANKIE: Beamish Irish Stout.

SAMUEL: I've been known to enjoy a good stout.

FRANKIE: Do you know this story? Pop? Does it sound familiar?

DASHIELL: Fuck, a hundred and sixty now. A hundred and sixty and getting higher.

FRANKIE: Dad? Dad?

SAMUEL: *(Lost)* Mmph?

FRANKIE: Do you know this story?

SAMUEL: I'd like to hear a story. Yes.

FRANKIE: How bout the one about the father who walks into a bar with his two sons? One of them is six, the other just turned three. Three bars in three days.

DASHIELL: A hundred and seventy, one-fuckin-seventy.

(JIMMYLARK *and* LADY ABIGAIL *begin to kiss.*)

SAMUEL: Can I have more wine?

(SAMUEL *holds out his glass—his hand shakes terribly.* FRANKIE *tries to pour him a glass.* SAMUEL*'s hand shakes too much.*)

DASHIELL: A hundred and eighty. A hundred and eighty and getting higher!

FRANKIE: Use your other hand. Both hands.

DASHIELL: It's getting worse.

FRANKIE: *(Gently)* Use both hands.

DASHIELL: No one will notice. No one will care.

FRANKIE: Like this, let me help— *(He tries to help—)*

SAMUEL: —I DON'T NEED HELP! I DON'T NEED HELP!

(JIMMYLARK and LADY ABIGAIL recline on the couch, continue to kiss, begin to grope.)

DASHIELL: *(Re: heart)* It's gonna explode. It's gonna explode.

(FRANKIE reaches out, gently puts his father's other hand on the glass.)

FRANKIE: Like that. Hold still. Hold still.

(SAMUEL doesn't resist FRANKIE's help. He holds the glass semi-steady as FRANKIE fills the glass half-way.)

DASHIELL: A hundred and ninety! A hundred and ninety-five! It's up to a hundred and ninety-five!

(SAMUEL manages to sip his wine using both hands to hold the glass. FRANKIE watches him, making sure he doesn't spill.)

SAMUEL: How long have you worked here?

FRANKIE: A long time.

SAMUEL: A long time. Yes. I remember.

DASHIELL: It's over two hundred! It's gonna burst!

(SAMUEL finishes his wine. He holds out his empty glass with one hand, it shakes.)

(FRANKIE gently moves his father's other hand onto the glass. He pours his father half a glass of wine.)

DASHIELL: It's gonna stop! It's gonna burst and then stop! Two hundred and twenty. Two hundred and thirty. No one will notice, no one will care.

SAMUEL: *(To FRANKIE)* Thank you.

DASHIELL: Two hundred and forty. Two hundred and fifty.

(SAMUEL *manages to sip his wine.* FRANKIE *stares at him.*)

(JIMMYLARK *and* LADY ABIGAIL *take off more and more clothes.*)

DASHIELL: I'm not gonna count anymore. I can't count. I'll wait. I'll just wait. Better not to know when. Better not to know. (*He stops looking at his watch, stops checking his pulse. He rocks back and forth, terrified, crying.*)

(SAMUEL *sips his wine.* FRANKIE *watches.*)

(JIMMYLARK *and* LADY ABIGAIL *begin to make love.*)

(*Silence, other than Mozart's* Violin Concerto #3...*as* JIMMYLARK *and* LADY ABIGAIL *have sex,* DASHIELL *cries, and* FRANKIE *watches* SAMUEL *drink, lost. Then...*)

BERRIAN: (*Very slowly, to no one in particular*) I dreamt of being a photographer. As a boy. Cameras... they interested me. I took photography classes... starting in...only the third grade. I learned apertures. Exposures. I learned how to develop my own film. In a dark room. You know...you can make a dark room almost anywhere. Out of almost anything. You can make a dark room without even having a room. You can put your hands inside a dark space and...feel around...for the film...the negative. Immersing it into the processing chemicals. Manipulating the image. You get good at it after awhile. With practice. (*Beat*) Black and white photos were my favorite. Still are. Color doesn't look right. Not quite. Not precisely. A form of false advertising. It wants to be real...but it's not real. It's a photograph. A snapshot. (*Beat*) Nina Wipranik was my first love. Nina Wipranik... is my true love. So pure. So innocent. I was in the third grade, she was in the fifth. Nina Wipranik. She was too pretty for me, sure. Of course she was. But she wasn't too pretty for my camera. No, I got some good shots of her. Snapshots. Action shots. Running and...hopping into a tree. Against a giant tree. One foot on the trunk, her

other foot in the air as she…twisted and…turned…
and hopped back to the ground. One…two…three…
four. Snap…snap…snap… snap. Oh, I must've taken
hundreds of her. Maybe thousands. Yes. It must have
been thousands. *(Beat)* I wonder if she ever knew.
(Beat) I wonder where she is now. What she's doing.
And who she's doing it with. *(Beat)* I think of her often.
Every day sometimes. Which is nice, I think. To have
someone to think of. *(Beat)* I think of her…fondly. I
look back on her…with fondness. *(A smile creeps in.)* I
should have said hello. Yes. I should have introduced
myself. I was in the third grade. She was in the fifth.
I shouldn't have let that stop me. *(Beat)* I should have
said hello. *(Beat)* I should have told her Hi. *(Beat)* I
wonder where she is. *(Beat)* I wonder what she's doing.
(Beat) Who she's doing it with. *(Beat)* I should have said
hello. *(Beat)* I should have introduced myself. *(Beat)*
Who's to say? *(Beat)* Who knows? *(Beat)* You never
know. *(Beat)* One…can never know.

(Mozart's Violin Concerto #3 *continues throughout.)*

*(*BERRIAN *watches* JIMMYLARK *and* LADY ABIGAIL *make
love.)*

*(*DASHIELL *rocks back and forth and cries in the corner—
once again looking at his watch, checking his pulse.)*

*(*FRANKIE *watches* SAMUEL *drink red wine.* SAMUEL's *mind
is somewhere else.)*

(Thirty seconds)

(Lights slowly fade to black)

END OF PLAY

THE BRONX TO THE `BU:
BRUCE LEONARD—WARTS AND ALL

BRUCE LEONARD—WARTS AND ALL was first presented by LAByrinth Theater Company (John Ortiz, Artistic Director), as part of the LAB25 festival on 20 September 2017, at Cherry Lane Theatre. The cast and creative contributor were:

BRUCE .... Chris McGarry

Director .... Brett C Leonard

CHARACTER & SETTING

BRUCE LEONARD

Present day

For my mother

(Lights up on:)

*(*BRUCE LEONARD*—severe lewy body dementia. Frail, weak, thin. His mind as deteriorated as his atrophied body. Present day)*

(On a small boombox we hear a smattering of applause. Then an M C says: "Bruce Leonard, how bout it? Bruce Leonard!")

(Then, in BRUCE's *own voice on the boombox: "You're gonna hear that name again—Bruce Leonard")*

(But on stage, BRUCE *remains motionless—in a nearly catatonic state. No movement of any kind.)*

(He remains motionless as…)

(We hear his voice singing something like Live Til I Die *on a small cassette player boombox. A terrific singer)*

(Also on the table is a D V D player, a second boombox that plays C Ds, a T V monitor, stacks of V H S tapes, D V Ds, C Ds, cassettes, pens, pencils and tissues.)

(He is wearing a baseball cap with a 4-leaf clover on the front. He wears a plaid robe, solid gray pajama bottoms and a gray T-shirt with a print of a 1950s microphone. He wears one comfortable old slipper.)

(A brass-handle cane rests against the table. A pile of dirty clothes on the ground near his feet.)

(Throughout the entirety of the song, he never speaks.)

(He doesn't move. He stares off in a catatonic state. Until…)

(When the song's tempo changes…his eyes slowly look down at the table before him…but he doesn't move…)

(He then gently, slowly, nudges a pen a little bit. Then…)

(Very slowly he begins to fold a piece of tissue into tiny squares. At an almost impossibly slow rate.)

(He then meticulously puts the folded tissue on the table.)

(Then looks at it. Stops. Stares at it)

(The song ends. He presses stop…or it ends on its own.)

(No more music. Silence)

BRUCE: Pretty good, Bruce.
Useta be pretty good.

(Silence)

(He stares at what he just made—the folded piece of tissue. Unsure if it is good or not. Unsure of what it is.)

(He nudges it a little bit. Then lifts it off the table and very slowly begins to unfold it as carefully as he folded it in the first place.)

(As he now speaks…very quietly…to himself…almost a mumble… Takes his time…long beats between each line…)

Hundred…
Hundred…
Minus seven…
Minus…
Hundred…minus…seven…
Equals…

(Pause)

Brown Derby…
Brown Derby…

(Pause)

Brown Derby
19…?

19...?

(Pause)

(He puts down the tissue paper. Stares at it. Nudges the pen toward the paper. Nudges the tissue and pen once again.)

(He looks at them.)

(Pause)

(He leans forward and presses play on the C D playing boombox. Something like Unchained Melody *is heard, once again sung by* BRUCE.*)*

(He begins to fold the tissue paper once again.)

(He stops and looks at the boombox playing the song. He listens intently. His focus and faculties very slowly coming back, just barely. But enough to notice that he sings the wrong lyrics on the boombox when he hears himself sing "cuz my love came to me.")

(After those incorrect lyrics, he then hears himself on the boombox speak the words "My son.")

(He holds down the rewind button on the C D player and we hear the audio reverse quickly, until he allows it to play once again.)

(And hears it again— "my son".)

(He rewinds again... He hears it again— "my son".)

(He rewinds again... He hears it again— "my son".)

(Rewinds...hears it— "my son".)

(Rewinds...hears it— "my son".)

(Rewinds...hears it— "my son".)

(He presses stop on the C D. Silence. He thinks. He tries to piece it together...tries to remember...with great difficulty... speaks softly...)

My son...
My son...

I have a...I have...I have a son.
A hundred minus seven...equals...
I have...I have a son...
Hundred minus seven...is ninety-three...minus
seven...eighty-six...
...A wife.
I have a wife...
Two sons...two sons...and a wife...
A wife...two sons...
I have a daughter...two sons...
And a wife...
My wife...
Barbara...
Barbara...
Barbara...

(He pronounces Barbara with all three syllables.)

(Pause)

Hundred minus seven is ninety-three...minus seven is
eighty-six...
Seventy-nine...

(Pause)

Barbara...

(Pause)

Barbara...

(Pause)

Bronx...
The Bronx... Born in The Bronx...New York...
New York...
Bronx, New York...
Teaneck...Teaneck High School...Teaneck, New
Jersey...
Rutgers University...class of...Rutgers, class of...

Minus seven is seventy-two...sixty-five...fifty-eight...
California
Brown Derby 1965, Class of '55
Barbara...Barbara and Bruce...
Fifty-four years
The Bronx to the 'Bu.

(Pause)

Minus seven is fifty-one...forty-four...thirty-seven...
I miss my wife...
I miss my wife...
I love my wife...
Barbara...
Fifty-four years...
Hello, Sweetheart...
Barbara. My life.
Brucie...Brett...Brigette...
Barbara.

(Pause)

I've missed you...Barbara...
I'll see you soon...
I'll be there soon...

(He presses play on the C D boombox and hears himself singing something like Fly Me To The Moon—*a capella at first.)*

(He listens.)

I'm on my way, Sweetheart.

(A piano begins to accompany him singing on the boombox. Here live...he slowly begins to prepare himself to go join Barbara.)

(He quietly sings along with himself on the stereo as he slowly finds a black leather sports coat in the pile of clothes. He takes off the robe and slips on the leather coat with a great

deal more ease and dexterity than we have previously seen— his memory, coordination and agility slowly coming back to him little by little. He puts on the other slipper that he finds under the pile of clothes.)

(On the boombox a band kicks in and begins to swing.)

(He sings along with himself a little louder now—his voice now that of a man some twenty to thirty years younger.)

(He finds a black fedora in the pile of clothes, takes off his baseball cap and smoothly flips the fedora onto his head.)

(He grabs the cane that's been leaning against the table, uses it more like Fred Astaire than like a crippled old man.)

(He dances a few smooth steps...a happy soft-shoe...)

(The music continues...as he looks toward the heavens...and spreads his arms as wide as the smile on his face...)

(...and finishes strong—now singing loudly, along with himself on the stereo...)

I said in other words...
Aw yes, in other words...
In other words...
I love you...

(Blackout)

(Applause on the boombox... We hear the announcer on the boombox say... "Ladies and gentlemen Bruce Leonard")

*(A large photo is projected of...*BRUCE LEONARD*, 80, a big smile across his face...)*

(...Posing with his black leather jacket, black fedora and brass-handled cane.)

END OF PLAY

WHAT I'M LOOKING FOR

WHAT I'M LOOKING FOR was first produced at Collaboraction's Sketchbook 2010 Festival (Anthony Moseley, Artistic Director) in Chicago, Illinois. The cast and creative contributors were:

FRANKIE...Joel Gross
TRACY .... Heather Bodie
CHOIR/ENSEMBLE .... Claire Tuft, Danielle LaVoy, Lauren Sivak, Leah Rose Orleans, Sarah Kinsey, Cheyenne Pinson, Claire Kander, Sheila O'Connor, Lillian Almaguer, Nora Taylor, Joan Merlo, Chris Conley, Joyce Porter, Alex Hugh Brown, Ben Kirberger, J P Pierson, Kevin Crispin, Nik Rokop, Peter Navis, Warren Lavon, Noe Jara, Marcus Kenyadi, Juan Lozada, Matthew LaChapelle

Band:
Piano .... Cliff Li
Violin ....Julia Merchant
Drums ....Don Marcus
Guitar.. Kevin Golden

Director .... Anthony Moseley
Assistant director..Nathan Green
Co-Producer ....Sarah Moeller
Set ....Sam Porretta
Lights .... Jeremy Getz
Costumes.. Katherine Stebbins
Props ....Steph Charaska
Casting... Two Birds Casting, Erica Sartini & Hanna Phenlon

CHARACTERS & SETTING

FRANKIE
TRACY
CHOIR/ENSEMBLE

A dark stage

WHAT I'M LOOKING FOR was inspired by
—*and with enormous thanks to*—
Rufus Wainwright's *Tower of Learning*

dedicated to Anthony Moseley

(A dark stage. Black)

(We hear, but cannot see FRANKIE *and* TRACY. *Calm but tense. Desperate. Then it grows. And grows. Until it explodes:)*

TRACY: Six years of my life…

FRANKIE: …Trace…

TRACY: …I can't…Frankie…I can't.

FRANKIE: Look at me…Tracy… Look at me…I will fucking…change…for you. I will change. What do you want me to do? Tell me what you want and I'll do it.

TRACY: I'm sorry.

FRANKIE: I love you.

TRACY: Don't…

FRANKIE: I said I love you.

TRACY: I know.

FRANKIE: I LOVE YOU!—

TRACY: —Stop—

FRANKIE: —WHAT ABOUT *MY* FUCKING LIFE?!—

TRACY: —Frankie, stop—

FRANKIE: —I FUCKING LOVE YOU!—

TRACY: —LOVE *HER*, FRANKIE, GO FUCK *HER*!!—

FRANKIE: *(Calm)* —Siddown, come here—

TRACY: —I AM DONE!!—

FRANKIE: *(Calm)* —Would you calm down for a sec—

TRACY: —DONE DONE DONE DONE DONE—

FRANKIE: —Stop it, siddown!!—

TRACY: —DONE DONE DONE DONE—

FRANKIE: —KNOCK IT OFF!—

TRACY: —DONE DONE DONE DONE DONE—

FRANKIE:—GET OVER HERE!—

TRACY: —DONE DONE DONE DONE DONE—

FRANKIE: —SHUT UP—

TRACY: —DONE DONE DONE DONE—

FRANKIE: —SHUT THE FUCK UP—

TRACY: —DONE DONE DONE—

FRANKIE: —WE'RE NOT DONE—

TRACY: —DONE DONE DONE DONE—

FRANKIE: —WE ARE NOT DONE—

TRACY: —DONE DONE DONE—

FRANKIE: —WOULD YOU SHUT THE FUCK UP?!—

TRACY: —DONE DONE DONE DONE—

FRANKIE: —WE WILL NEVER BE DONE!—

TRACY: —DONE DONE DONE DONE DONE DONE DONE DONE…Frankie, no, FRANKIE!—

FRANKIE: —I LOVE YOU!

(We hear a strange, dull noise. A knife piercing clothes and flesh.)

FRANKIE: I love you…

TRACY: *(Another dull noise)* Please…

FRANKIE: …I love you.

TRACY: *(Another dull noise)* No…

(Another dull noise)

TRACY: Frankie... *(Soft)* Please...

(Another dull noise.)

(A very long silence on the black stage. Then...quietly...)

FRANKIE: Baby?... *(Beat, soft)* Baby? *(Beat, soft)* Tracy? *(Beat, soft)* Trace... *(Beat, soft)* Tracy... *(Beat, soft)* No... Please... *(Beat, soft)* No... No...Tracy...I love you.

(Long silence... stage remains black...5-10 seconds... then:)

(A piano is heard live offstage. Playing softly. Something like Rufus Wainwright's Tower of Learning. *The opening chords play over and over again, until, eventually...)*

(The lights very slowly rise to reveal FRANKIE... *splattered with blood. He is sitting in a chair, a bloody knife in his hand.)*

(On the ground at his feet is TRACY...*dead. Covered in blood. Stabbed in the chest. In her heart.)*

(The piano continues as FRANKIE *softly sings to her...)*

(The piano continues.)

(Remaining on the ground, TRACY *slowly lifts her head and sings. They look into one another's eyes. [The lyrics are also sung softly by an offstage* CHOIR*])*

*(*TRACY *sings.)*

(The CHOIR *hums offstage...)*

(A few more offstage musicians join the pianist...as lights very slowly reveal a CHOIR.*)*

(One of every two CHOIR *members holds a "murder" weapon. Those choir members who DO NOT hold instruments of death are the victims of those they stand beside.)*

(These "couples" include, but are not limited to, the following:)

*(1. MARRIED COUPLE. He is in pajamas, she is in a
nightgown. Old bruises and marks on her arms and face. She
shot him in his sleep with a 9MM handgun.)*

*(2. BOYFRIEND/GIRLFRIEND in House Moving Clothes, bits
of paint on their hands and clothes. They have been painting
the inside of their new condo. He killed her with a small can
of paint, multiple blows to the side of her head.)*

*(3. BROTHER/SISTER wearing black suit/tie, black dress.
After their parents' funeral. Tear-stained cheeks. She killed
him with their father's antique pistol. Two shots to the chest,
one to the face.)*

*(4. MOTHER/SON. SON is in his pajamas, has Down's
Syndrome. MOTHER is in a pant-suit. She holds a large
empty bottle of prescription pills. It is unclear if she killed
him or he killed himself. Either way she should be crippled
with guilt.)*

*(5. FATHER/DAUGHTER. FATHER is in his boxers. No shirt,
no shoes. DAUGHTER is in a nightgown. DAUGHTER holds a
shotgun or rifle. FATHER has been shot in the chest.)*

*(6. MOTHER/DAUGHTER. A hospital. MOTHER is in a
hospital gown, skinny, pale, weak. DAUGHTER holds a
pillow, the pillow she used to suffocate her ailing mother.
Euthanasia)*

*(7. NEWLYWEDS. He is in bow-tie, cummerbund, tux shirt,
tux pants. She is in a wedding dress, one high heel, one bare
foot. He hit her in the head with a champagne bottle.)*

*(8. HUSBAND/WIFE or BOYFRIEND/GIRLFRIEND. He is
just home from work, still in his fast-food uniform. She is
in a short dress, heels, hair and face done, was getting ready
to go out on the town. She has bruises around her neck. He
strangled her and suffocated her with a plastic take-out bag
from his work.)*

*(9. HUSBAND/WIFE. They were sitting in front of the fire,
relaxing, romantic. Appropriately comfortable clothes. Cozy.*

In for the night, cold outside. He killed her with a fireplace poker, multiple blows to the head.)

(10. YOUNG BROTHER/SISTER. They were playing with Daddy's gun. It went off. BROTHER was shot in chest.)

(11. MODEL/PHOTOGRAPHER. She is in a bikini. He is in jeans, polo shirt, loafers. He was taking "modeling" pictures of her in the woods, near a lake. Perhaps he should have a camera around his neck. He strangled her with his belt or camera strap. Her hands should be tied behind her back.)

(12. BOYFRIEND/GIRLFRIEND. He's stoned, wears sweatpants, dirty white socks without shoes, a white V-neck T-shirt with yellow underarm stains. She is hard-working, well-dressed, recently home from a hard day's work at the office. She's an architect or a lawyer. She's still in her work clothes, but no shoes. Her feet were sore. She killed him with a large kitchen knife. She went from slicing vegetables to slashing his face and throat.)

(As the music continues FRANKIE takes TRACY's hand. They rise. They look into each others' eyes as…)

(FRANKIE sings.)

(FRANKIE and CHOIR sing.)

(FRANKIE sings.)

(FRANKIE and CHOIR sing.)

(The CHOIR begins to walk downstage…slowly, elegantly as…)

(FRANKIE and TRACY sing.)

(FRANKIE, TRACY and CHOIR sing.)

(FRANKIE sings.)

(The CHOIR members begin to dance. Each killer with his/ her victim. A waltz. All in unison, in perfect synch. A dance of death. Slow. Elegant. Beautiful)

(FRANKIE sings to TRACY.)

(The music continues. The dance of death continues.
FRANKIE *and* TRACY *join in the waltz. Everyone dances.*
Paired in sets of two. They do not sing. They do not hum.
They simply dance…each looking into the eyes of his/her
victim or killer.)

(The musicians continue to play.)

(Eventually…)

*(*TRACY *moves slowly away from* FRANKIE. *Back to her*
original position on the ground. Dead. FRANKIE *remains…*
staring at her.)

(The dead members of each "couple" slowly move away from
their partners. The living ones remain…still…motionless…
watching as the dead disappear into black or offstage.)

(The music continues.)

*(*FRANKIE *moves slowly toward* TRACY. *He stands above*
her…the knife still in his hand. His back to the audience.)

(The music continues.)

(The killers slowly move toward the location of their victims'
exits/disappearances. Moments before disappearing or
exiting, each killer drops his/her instrument of death. They
then disappear into black or offstage.)

*(*FRANKIE *drops the knife.)*

(The music continues.)

*(*FRANKIE *sits in the chair,* TRACY *on the ground near his*
feet.)

(5-10 seconds of music. Then…the music ends.)

(Silence)

(30-90 seconds of silence)

(The lights very, very slowly fade to black.)

END OF PLAY

BOBO AN' SPYDER AN' A GIRL FROM DOWN UNDER

BOBO AN' SPYDER AN' A GIRL FROM DOWN UNDER was commissioned by The Production Company (Artisitic Director, Mark Armstrong) and produced in New York City in 2006. The cast and creative contributor were:

BOBO .... Salvatore Inzerillo
SPYDER .... Chris McGorry
SAM .... Nicolle Bradford

Director .... Bob Glaudini

CHARACTERS & SETTING

BOBO
SPYDER
SAM

New York City. The present.

(New York City. The Present.)

(Lights up on BOBO *and* SPYDER, *40+ yr. old males with arrested development.)*

*(*BOBO *alternates from his marijuana pipe to his bong, as high as he's ever been. Or rather, as high as he's always been. He hasn't been "low" in almost twenty-seven years.)*

*(*SPYDER *drinks from his fourth 40-oz "Country Club" malt liquor of the day. He drinks. It's what he does. A strong believer in sticking to what one does best.)*

(Something like The Clash's I'm So Bored With the U S A *blasts through the oversized, most-likely-stolen speakers in this run-down, fucked-up, hole-in-the-wall, Lower East Side railroad-apartment.)*

*(*BOBO *smokes.)*

*(*SPYDER *drinks.)*

(They don't look at each other.)

(They don't tap their toes, or snap their fingers, or bob their heads.)

(They smoke and drink.)

(It's almost as if there isn't any music at all.)

(It's almost as if each man sits alone.)

(The song comes to an end. They sat silent and virtually motionless—with the exception of occasionally smoking and drinking—throughout the entire playing time.)

(Something like The Clash's Cheat *begins. Before any lyrics are sung:)*

BOBO: *(Re: the song)* I like this one.

SPYDER: This a good one.

*(*BOBO *and* SPYDER *don't look at each other, or tap their toes, or snap their fingers, or bob their heads.)*

(They drink and smoke. In silence)

*(*BOBO *lights a regular tobacco cigarette—a Pall Mall.* SPYDER *looks over and makes a subtle gesture, requesting a cigarette from* BOBO. BOBO *tosses the pack to* SPYDER. *It hits* SPYDER *in the face and drops to the floor. No biggie—* SPYDER *picks it up. He takes a cigarette out of the pack and lights up, using a match from a book on the cluttered, filthy coffee table before him.)*

*(*BOBO *alternates between his bong and his Pall Mall.* SPYDER *alternates between his 40oz. and his Pall Mall.)*

(At some point during "Cheat" the music suddenly stops.)

(Silence)

(And more silence…as BOBO *and* SPYDER *sit motionless, seemingly unaffected.)*

(Until…)

SPYDER: I was startin' ta get inta that. *(Pause. He shrugs, he drinks.)*

BOBO: Me too.

(Pause)

*(*BOBO *slowly moves off the easy chair, down to the floor, on all fours, and literally crawls to the stereo. He presses eject on the cassette-deck. He removes a stretched-out, un-spooled, homemade tape of The Clash.* BOBO *stares at it. He simply stares, emotionless. He seems clueless as to what to do next.* SPYDER *pays him no mind.)*

(Pause)

*(Finally…*BOBO *attempts to "re-spool" the tape by rotating his finger in one of the holes.)*

(He doesn't make much progress. He stops and stares at the tape.)

(Pause)

BOBO: He need ta get'isself a C D player.

SPYDER: He need ta get'is cheap-ass a lotta shit. This place's a fuckin' dump.

(Pause)

*(*BOBO *once again tries to re-spool the tape. Not a lotta success. He stops.)*

(He nonchalantly tosses the tape across the room—it hits a wall.)

(Long pause)

*(*BOBO *crawls back to his pipe. Inhales. Exhales.* SPYDER *continues to drink. Silence. Until...)*

BOBO: I'm hungry. *(Beat)* You hungry? *(Beat)* I'm starved.

(No response. BOBO *smokes. Pause)*

SPYDER: We should steal one.

BOBO: Pizza?

SPYDER: A C D player. Gotta steal one. Can't be waitin' on his ass ta get nuthin', off chasin' skirt round the globe, wherever. *(Beat)* Faggot.

BOBO: He don't got no D V D player neither.

(Beat)

SPYDER: No MP3.

(Beat)

BOBO: No Playstation.

SPYDER: This dick fly all o'er the world a pair a' tits an' a smile, can't afford a unbroken boombox.

BOBO: He cheap, bro.

SPYDER: Skirt-chasin'-fag.

BOBO: Cheap-ass-bitch.

SPYDER: Lil' dick prick.

(*Beat*)

BOBO: It's good he ain't chargin' us ta stay here, though.

SPYDER: For what?

BOBO: I dunno, y'know…sometimes when people move in? Like a sublet?

SPYDER: He ain't here, shit, that homo's off chasin' pussy halfway 'cross the globe, why he gonna charge us shit? 'Sides, we could water his plants if he had some. He's *lucky* we're here, burglary an' shit? Man, they got C D players in fuckin' *rehab*, bro—this cassette only shit es no bueno, serious.

BOBO: They got C D players in Bellevue, too. They got a big-ass movie room also. Showin' all *kinda* good shit—*new releases*. Fuckin' *surround* sound! T H X X 5-point-one *Dolby*, bro—*Dolby*! Livin' *large* in fuckin' Bellevue, bro, belie' that! Believe it.

(*Beat.* BOBO *smokes.*)

SPYDER: You a stoner, bro.

BOBO: I like how it makes me feel.

SPYDER: You been like stoned since you like come out the vagina, huh?

BOBO: I dunno. I don' remember comin' out the vagina. That was a long time ago.

SPYDER: You stupid, man.

BOBO: You stupid.

SPYDER: Where'd I put that Booster Bag at? You seen where I put that shit? Huh? Bobo?

BOBO: I dunno.

SPYDER: It ain't over by you somewhere? Sittin' on it with your fat ass?

BOBO: I ain't sittin' on it. I am hungry, though, you ain't hungry? My fuckin' stomach startin' ta hurt.

SPYDER: I find that Booster Bag? We find that shit? This place be like a "P C Richard *Holiday* Sale" his ass get back home chasin' titty. Have like, fuckin'...D V D player, plasma flat screen, that lil' whaddaya call, computer-thing?, where ya like fold it under your arm an' shit, in like a lil' man-bag? A *laptop*! Have a fuckin' laptop up in this shit. His ass get home? —fuckin' *surprise*, bro—new C D player, boombox, T V—

BOBO: —Playstation?

SPYDER: Playstation, hell yeah—Madden N F L, Grand Theft Auto—

BOBO: —We gotta get some pornos too.

SPYDER: Porno, yeah, fuck yeah, get some porn up in this mothafucka, take turns, five minutes me, five minutes you, we'll go in like *innervals*—*shifts*—I go, you go, I go. I ain't goin' the same time as you bro, fuck that shit.

BOBO: I don' wanna do that.

SPYDER: Yeah, right, you be all lookin' over an' shit, comparin' jackhammers.

BOBO: I wouldn't look, *you'd* prolly look.

SPYDER: I wouldn't, shit, you would.

BOBO: Why would I wanna look? Fuck you.

(Beat)

SPYDER: Curiosity.

BOBO: Wha'?

SPYDER: You're the one doin' the lookin', ask your own self.

BOBO: I ain't lookin'.

SPYDER: But you would prolly is what I'm sayin'—cuz a' the curiosity.

BOBO: I'm not curious.

SPYDER: I'm juss sayin' I'd understand if you did, that's all.

BOBO: But I wouldn't.

SPYDER: And I respect that, I do. I'm juss sayin'… *(Beat)* Be normal if ya did, no big deal.

(SPYDER drinks. BOBO stares at him. Beat)

BOBO: Dude?

SPYDER: What?

BOBO: I don't wanna see your dick.

SPYDER: I didn't say you *did*. I said "*if*".

BOBO: I just wanna eat a pizza.

SPYDER: I apologize.

BOBO: I'm starvin'.

SPYDER: I'm not responsible for my words or actions when I'm drunk.

BOBO: You're always drunk.

SPYDER: An' thusly never responsible.

(Knock-knock-knock-knock-knock on the front door.)

SPYDER: They've come with my straight jacket—42 long.

(Knock-knock-knock-knock-knock)

WOMAN'S VOICE: *(O S. With an Australian accent)* Tony? Tony, are you there?

(*Knock-knock-knock*)

WOMAN'S VOICE: *(O S)* Tony? I can smell the smoke, open up.

(BOBO *and* SPYDER *put out their cigarettes and the pipe—they try to wave away the smoke...as:*)

WOMAN'S VOICE: *(O S)* Please...Tone...I'm sorry. Did you hear me? I said I was sorry. I made a mistake, you were right. I *lied* to you. Can you hear me? I love you. I lied when I said I didn't. Please. I've come to tell you in person. I love you. Tone... Open up. Please. I love you.

(BOBO *opens the door.*)

BOBO: I love you too.

SPYDER: Yeah, me too.

BOBO: You don't got pizza with you by any chance, do ya?

(*Outside the door is* SAM *[Samantha], a twenty-something woman in jeans, cowboy boots, a white tank-top.*)

SAM: No, I... (*She re-checks the apartment number on the door.*) Is this...this is 2114 Rivington? Yes? Does Tony Barton live here? Anthony Barton? I'm Sam. Samantha. Are you friends of his? Yes? Maybe you've heard of me.

SPYDER: Maybe not.

SAM: Is this where he lives? Please—do I have the right apartment? Did he move? Yes? No?

BOBO: He's not home right now.

SPYDER: But you're welcome ta stay n' join us if ya' like—we're nice people.

SAM: So this *is* his apartment? I'm in the right place?

SPYDER: We're here ta water his plants.

SAM: Do you know when he'll be back? Do you have any idea?

(BOBO *shrugs, then looks to* SPYDER.)

SPYDER: Ya sure ya don' wanna join us for a drink, sweetheart? *(He holds up his 40oz.)*

BOBO: *(To* SAM*)* I don't drink.

SPYDER: Take a lil' visit ta the "Country Club"? Nuthin' but the best for you, kid, anything. *(He drinks.)*

BOBO: Spyder's an alcoholic.

SPYDER: I'm pretty good at sex, too.

SAM: Would you mind if I left him a message—a note? I'm, uh…I'm a very close friend of his.

SPYDER: A friend a' his, a friend a' mine. Have a drink, sweetheart, grab yourself a forty outta the fridge.

SAM: No, I—

SPYDER: —Ah, come on, ya never know—he could be home any minute.

SAM: Where did he go?

SPYDER: How do we know you ain't the Po-Po?

SAM: The what?

SPYDER: Su casa es mi casa, comprendo?

BOBO: Entre-vouz, Madamemoiselle.

SPYDER: We're lovely people.

BOBO: Make yourself at home.

SPYDER: We have.

(*After a brief hesitation,* SAM *enters slowly, with a suitcase in her hand. She knows this is Tony's place. Apparently* BOBO *and* SPYDER *know him. She wants answers.*)

SAM: I'd like to leave a short note…I just wanna —

SPYDER: —Got designs on spendin' the night, kid? *(Pats the empty space next to him)* You can use my lap as a pillow.

SAM: *(To* BOBO*)* Do you have something I can write on? It doesn't haveta—

SPYDER: —I got somethin', yeah—might not be exactly what ya had in mind, but I'm game if you are.

*(*SAM *looks at* SPYDER. *He shrugs and drinks.* BOBO *rips the edge off a pizza box and hands it to her.)*

BOBO: Here ya go.

SAM: Thank you.

SPYDER: You're welcome—now get over here an' take a load off. *(He drinks.)*

*(*SAM *takes a pen out of her purse and begins to write.)*

*(*BOBO *shuts the door, then sits on the floor with his pipe.)*

*(*SAM *stops writing. A bit nervously, she looks to the closed door—then to* BOBO *and* SPYDER.*)*

BOBO: *(Offering the pipe)* You smoke?

SAM: No.

SPYDER: C'mon, have a seat.

*(*SAM *looks over at* SPYDER, *who drinks while patting his thigh for her to come sit. She goes back to her note.)*

SPYDER: I'll keep it warm for ya.

*(*SPYDER *drinks.* BOBO *smokes.* SAM *writes.)*

SPYDER: Ahh, c'mon, join me, will ya? What're ya' doin' over there anyway, writin' a *novel*? Last book your friend Tony read was "Hundred Ways To Suck A Dick".

BOBO: *(Lungs full of smoke)* I read the Willis Reed biography.

SAM: *(Re: the note)* I'm gonna leave it right here, okay? No—I'll leave it over here on the refrigerator—I don't want it to get lost with all this other stuff.

(It takes four magnets to make the thick cardboard stick, as she continues:)

SAM: This is very important, do you understand? I left my email address, in case he's misplaced it, it's all in the note. Please—tell him I'll be checking as often as possible, I don't have a computer but I'll find someplace—an internet café—maybe the hotel when I find a one—I don't know where I'm staying yet—I was planning…I was *hoping*.

SPYDER: I ain't gonna stop ya.

SAM: It's all written down right here. It's right here on the fridge.

BOBO: He ain't even got a C D player.

SAM: Just make sure he gets it please.

BOBO: *(Lungs full of smoke)* Cheap-ass-bitch.

SPYDER: Skirt-chasin'-fag.

SAM: Please. It's very important. Please.

(SAM moves for the front door. She's stopped with:)

SPYDER: Hey, love, do me a favor, huh? —while you're up? —grab me another forty outta the fridge, could ya? It'd be much appreciated.

(Pause… She looks at SPYDER, but does not move for the refrigerator.)

SPYDER: C'mon. We'll make sure he gets the note. I promise. Pretty please. I'm almost finished this one.

(SAM hesitates a beat, then goes to the fridge and takes out a forty. She walks over to SPYDER and puts it on the coffee table in front of him.)

SPYDER: Thank you.

SAM: Thank you.

(SPYDER *"pats" the empty space next to him.*)

SPYDER: There really is no need for a hotel, ya know?

SAM: *(Moves to exit)* I'll check my email as often as possible.

(SAM *picks up her suitcase. As she passes by* BOBO, *he once again offers her the pipe.*)

BOBO: Some'n for the road, maybe?

SAM: Thank you—no. Remember the note. Goodbye. *(She exits and shuts the door behind her.)*

SPYDER: Come on back, cowgirl. Giddy-on-up, Spyder style.

(BOBO *looks at* SPYDER. SPYDER *simulates* SAM *riding him cowgirl style.*)

SPYDER: Ride-'em, slide-'em cowgirl. *(As if "smacking" her ass)* P'kssh, p'kssh. Yee-haw. *(He stops suddenly, seemingly no longer interested in sex. He drinks.)*

(Pause)

BOBO: She was from England.

SPYDER: Mph?

BOBO: You called'r "cowgirl".

SPYDER: So?

BOBO: England don't have no cows.

SPYDER: She had cowboy boots. She was alright, right?, nice kid. Go on, read the note. When we steal that laptop?, we gonna email'r. We'll invite'r for pizza.

BOBO: Pepperoni an' anchovies?

SPYDER: Whatever ya want, why not? *(To himself)* Porn an' pizza.

(As BOBO *slowly rises and moves to the fridge:)*

BOBO: And olives. Pepperoni, anchovies, and olives. And sausage. Sausage is the shit. *(He removes the pizza box note from the fridge.)* She has nice handwriting.

SPYDER: Hurry up, I gotta piss.

BOBO: *(Reading)* "Tony. I came all this way to look into your eyes and have you in my arms once again." *(Stops reading and looks up) Dude…*

SPYDER: C'mon, go on.

BOBO: *(Reading)* "I wanted to surprise you."

SPYDER: Surprise!

BOBO: "I wanted to tell you `I love you'. I *do* love you. I love you, Tony." *(Stops reading)* I can't, bro.

SPYDER: Juss finish it, c'mon, I gotta pee.

BOBO: Shit is fruity. *(Reading)* "I'm not afraid anymore. I've left Australia behind for good." *(Stops reading.) Australia?*

SPYDER: I dunno, keep reading.

BOBO: Where Tony at chasin' that girl he like? He went ta Australia, he said?

SPYDER: Naw, Austria, I think—he din't go ta no Australia, man—c'mon—make sure her e-mail's legible—she was cute, right? Cowboy boots, real flirty.

BOBO: Aus-*tria*? Not Aus-*tralia*?

SPYDER: Yeah, man, fuck, c'mon—he said he's chasin' some girl he left behind lived in Aus-*tria*. Europe. Now go on, Read the letter, my bladder's about ta explode.

BOBO: This chick was from England, I don't care what her note says.

SPYDER: Exactly.

BOBO: I seen every James Bond, I'm good about accents, bro. Prolly somewheres around London. Manchester maybe.

SPYDER: Terrific.

BOBO: Or Liverpool—she sounded like Ringo Starr.

(As SPYDER *rises for the first time in the play and slowly makes his way toward the bathroom:)*

SPYDER: I gotta piss—don't lose that email—there was definitely somethin' goin' on there between us—a lil' some'n-some'n in the eyes—lil' spark. I know Australia, too. I know that shit. Kangaroos. Mel Gibson. I know all a' that shit. Rugby. *(He exits into the bathroom.)*

*(*BOBO *reads the rest of the note, silently.)*

(We hear SPYDER *peeing offstage.)*

*(*BOBO *drops the note on the filthy, littered, cluttered counter.)*

(He lights up his pipe.)

(He smokes.)

(He takes his place on the floor.)

*(*SPYDER *continues with the world's longest pee.)*

(The Clash's I'm So Bored With the U S A *is heard as the lights slowly fade to black.)*

END OF PLAY

REBUTTAL

REBUTTAL was first presented at LAByrinth Theater Company's Summer Intensive, 2012 (Artistic Directors, Stephen Adly Guirgis, Mimi O'Donnell & Yul Vázquez). The cast and creative contributor were:

HECTOR .... Carlo Alban
MARY .... Elizabeth Canavan
CHRISTOPHER .... Kevin Geer
JOSS .... Paola Lazaro-Munoz

Director .... Brett C Leonard

CHARACTERS & SETTING

HECTOR
MARY
CHRISTOPHER
JOSS

A stage of scattered furniture strewn about

(Lights up on two men and two women. They sit on a stage of scattered furniture strewn about, overturned. Chairs on their sides, tables with legs toward the ceiling.)

(They are each sitting. Separate. Each one of them is alone, disconnected.)

(All of them extremely bored. Tired)

(Then…)

HECTOR: Blah…blah…blah…blah…blah… *(Beat)* Blah.

(Beat)

MARY: Wah-wah-wah-wah-wah—

CHRISTOPHER: Chatter chatter chatter—

JOSS: Ramble ramble ramble—

(HECTOR makes the sound of raspberries.)

MARY: *(Sing songs)* Love is love is love is love…

(HECTOR makes the sound of raspberries.)

(CHRISTOPHER makes a fart sound with his mouth.)

JOSS: Wall to wall—

CHRISTOPHER: Non-stop.

MARY: *(Sing songs)* If I can't have you, then I will kill you—

CHRISTOPHER: *(Sing songs)* I'm so alone my heart is breaking.

JOSS: *(Sings as melodramatic southern belle)* I'm so alone my heart is broken.

(HECTOR *makes the sound of raspberries.*)

(MARY *makes a fart sound with her mouth.*)

CHRISTOPHER: *(Sarcastic)* Let's all say what's on our mind.

MARY: *(Rhyming w/*CHRISTOPHER*)* In your case, Chris, you'll have plenty of time.

CHRISTOPHER: In my case?

HECTOR: You heard her.

MARY: My name is Mary.

HECTOR: Yes, ma'am.

MARY: Si, señor.

CHRISTOPHER: *(Sarcastic)* Let's say exactly what's on our minds! No subtext necessary!

(JOSS *makes the sound of raspberries.*)

(HECTOR *"farts" with his hand under his armpit.*)

CHRISTOPHER: *(Sings:)* I'll say what's on my mind, it will leave lots of time, to…discuss other things, while…I can simply sing and sing—

JOSS: *(Sings)* Because we are, what we are…we are, we are—

MARY: *(Sings)* We are, we are…we are—

HECTOR: *(Sings)* What we are, we behave to gain, to gain, to gain— *(Now speaks like a preacher)* NO! To impress! To yearn for!—

MARY: *(Mocking)* "He writes so good."

JOSS: So "well".

MARY: "He writes so well."

HECTOR: Yes, he really is such a good writer.

MARY: Very impressive.

CHRISTOPHER: What a wide variety of characters he is able to capture.

MARY: Or she.

CHRISTOPHER: Yes, or she.

JOSS: Very impressive.

HECTOR: And entertaining! Entertaining most of all!!

MARY: That's the goal.

HECTOR: The end all, be all.

JOSS: *(Hands to the sky)* Wheee....

MARY: *(Hands to the sky)* Wheee....

ALL: *(Together. Hands to the sky)* Wheee...

MARY: Here comes the corckscrew. Wheee...

ALL: *(Together)* Wheee...

CHRISTOPHER: Whoa, that was awesome.

HECTOR: Wheee, that was awesome.

JOSS: That was motherfuckin' fuckin fuckin off the chain yo, word yo, to the izzle my nizzle my pussy juss drizzled cuz I'm a cursin' urban nigga like the peeps like ta peep on they cultural tourist guide vacation time on the Q T, D L, first hit's free rhyme—wheee!!!!!

ALL: *(Together)* Wheee!!!!!!!!!!!!!

MARY: Word.

CHRISTOPHER: Word.

HECTOR: Word.

JOSS: Shit, mothafuckas, shit, cock cunt fuck poopoo jism penis whore, and y'all can say dat again!

HECTOR: Word.

CHRISTOPHER: Word.

MARY: Word up!

(They all make the raspberry sound.)

(They all fart with their arms.)

(MARY lifts a leg and farts with her ass.)

(CHRISTOPHER does the same.)

(HECTOR and JOSS do the same.)

(They all fart. And fart again. And fart again.)

(Then each makes the sound of raspberries.)

(MARY begins to drool on herself. Drool running down her chin, onto her neck, dripping onto her shirt.)

(As JOSS begins to cry—tears running down her face. Snot)

(HECTOR begins juggling three balls he gets from his pockets.)

(CHRISTOPHER stands and tap dances.)

(This goes on for awhile, until…)

(MARY stops drooling on herself and tries to upstage CHRISTOPHER by break dancing in front of him.)

(CHRISTOPHER turns up the urgency—tap dances faster and faster. CHRISTOPHER and MARY vie for attention.)

(JOSS's tears, sobs and wails get louder and more severe.)

(HECTOR continues juggling as he begins to sing Ave Maria.)

(The others continue to dance, break dance, cry.)

(HECTOR stops juggling, but continues to sing "Ave Maria"…as he pulls down his pants, squats, readies himself to take a shit on stage. He grunts and strains—while still singing—as he forces his bowels to move.)

(The others stop what they're doing and turn to face him.)

(HECTOR continues to grunt and force. And sing.)

(He shits on stage while he sings Ave Maria.)

(The other three turn toward the audience—they stare out. They look from left to right, right to left. Everywhere and anywhere but toward HECTOR.*)*

*(*HECTOR *stops singing. He pulls up his pants.)*

(The other three try to "play it off", as if the audience isn't there, or somehow didn't notice. CHRISTOPHER *twiddles his thumbs.* MARY *nonchalantly whistles to herself.* JOSS *mindlessly picks invisible lint from her clothes.)*

(They casually return to their chairs. They sit.)

*(*HECTOR *remains on his feet, addresses each of them as they ignore him—going through the above mentioned behaviors.)*

HECTOR: What? *(Beat)* What? *(Beat)* That's right, bitches, that's right. Es correcto y muy bueno! *(He grabs a handful of shit and offers it to the others.)* Come mi caca! Come mi caca! *(Faces audience with the shit still in his hand)* COME MI CACA! YA THINK THAT'S EASY? HUH? YOU TRY SHITTIN' ON CUE! *(Suddenly speaks to the audience like a pirate with a patch over his eye)* I have come to rape your women. How much? How much gold to rape your little girls? That one there—the little itty bitty baby in your arms, on your titty—the itty bitty bitty on your titty. Arrghh. Arrghh. *(Speaks like British royalty)* Would you like to join me for a spot of tea and a biscuit?

*(*JOSS *stands, speaks like an uneducated southerner.)*

JOSS: Gots me some swee'tea 'joy on da bench-swing 'neath da moonlight wi'cha if yuz wan'?

*(*MARY *leaps to her feet!)*

MARY: Objection your honor, this is an innocent man! Our system is built upon the foundation 'tis better for nine guilty men to taste freedom than for one innocent man to experience the incarcerated taste of cock up his ass!

CHRISTOPHER: Overruled!

(HECTOR *bends over as* JOSS *begins to fuck him from behind.*)

HECTOR: But I am an innocent man!

JOSS: Not no more ya ain't, cracka!

(JOSS *fucks* HECTOR, *as* CHRISTOPHER *taps* JOSS *on the shoulder.*)

CHRISTOPHER: May I cut in?

JOSS: Gimme another minute.

(JOSS *continues fucking* HECTOR *in the ass.* CHRISTOPHER *waits his turn.* MARY *gets in line behind* CHRISTOPHER. *Then* CHRISTOPHER *fucks* JOSS…*while* MARY *fucks* CHRISTOPHER…*as they all sing, including* HECTOR:)

ALL: *(Together. Sing)*
We're not fact, we're just fiction
No points of view
To offer you
Except the ones that we were given…

(*Suddenly, a quick change of tone…as* HECTOR *straightens up and throws the balls he was juggling at* CHRISTOPHER, JOSS *and* MARY. *Along with other balls he keeps pulling from his many pockets. Ball after ball after ball after ball. They retreat upstage, against the back wall, ducking, dodging, trying to block the attack. As* HECTOR *yells at them:)*

HECTOR: WHAT'S GOIN' ON, MAN?! HOW'S LIFE, MAN?! FUCKIN' A, RIGHT, MAN! FUCKIN' B-C-D, MAN! LIFE IS A SERIES OF EVENTS THAT NEVER STOPS, MAN, UNTIL IT STOPS, MAN, AND UNTIL IT STOPS IT GOES ON AND ON AND ON AND ON AND ON AND ON AND ON AND ON AND ON AND ON AND ON AND ON AND ON

AND ON AND ON AND ON AND ON AND ON
AND ON AND ON AND ON!!

(HECTOR's *thrown the last of the balls. Many of the balls
hit the others, resulting in cries of…"that doesn't hurt", "it
doesn't hurt", "you can't hurt us", "if you're trying to hurt
us, you can't hurt us!", "we don't hurt", "why should we
hurt?".)*

(Until… on the very last ball:)

CHRISTOPHER: OW!!! *(Holding his arm, whines)* Why'd ya
haveta go an' do that for? Shiiiittt…

MARY: *(Rubbing her arm)* Fuck.

JOSS: *(Rubbing her thigh)* Fuckyfuck.

MARY: Fuckyfucky.

HECTOR: What's the good word, Larry Bird?
Black man, brown man, red man, yellow man.

JOSS: *(English accent—no longer rubbing her thigh)* I
passed through the town square and couldn't help but
notice an abandoned and exiled young lady bathing
sans clothing in the midst of a fountain.

MARY: *(English accent, no longer rubbing her arm)* The
midst of the fountain and the mist of the fountain. *(She
laughs.)*

JOSS: Midst and mist, yes, ha-ha, midst and mist.

(JOSS and MARY continue to laugh and laugh.)

(CHRISTOPHER and HECTOR make the sound of raspberries.)

(Suddenly…lights rise on a kitchen sink, upstage.)

*(They all turn and stare at it. No more laughing, no more
raspberries.)*

(Long pause)

MARY: Is that dripping or leaking?

CHRISTOPHER: I think it's dripping.

JOSS: It's leaking.

HECTOR: It doesn't exist.

(They continue to stare at it.)

(Then, in unison, they all slowly turn and look at the audience.)

(Pause. They try to speak discreetly.)

MARY: They're watching it.

CHRISTOPHER: They're staring at it.

JOSS: Mesmerized.

HECTOR: Assholes.

CHRISTOPHER: Pricks.

MARY: Cocksuckers.

JOSS: Jerks. Fucking…fucking—

MARY: —dildos.

(They continue to look at the audience. They slowly look over their shoulders at the sink. Then back toward the audience.)

HECTOR: Ignore it. Smile.

(They all smile.)

(Pause)

(Through their smiling teeth:)

MARY: No one's watching us.

HECTOR: Keep smiling.

(Pause)

JOSS: No one's watching us.

HECTOR: Keep. Fucking. Smiling.

(Pause)

CHRISTOPHER: No one's paying any attention to us.

MARY: How could they? Look at that sink.

Joss: It's beautiful.

Mary: Gorgeous.

Christopher: What a beautiful, gorgeous, entertaining sink.

Hector: IGNORE THE FUCKIN' SINK!

(They all look at Hector. *He gets an idea.)*

Hector: Hurry, we gotta move it.

Christopher: It's too big.

Hector: WE GOTTA MOVE IT!!!!!!

*(*Hector *moves upstage for the sink. He tries to move it, shove it, lift it…as the others stay where they are, watching.)*

Hector: *(To the others)* C'mon! *(He continues to struggle with it…)* Uuuggghhhhh!!!!!!!!! *(Stops)* Fuck.

Christopher: It's too big.

Hector: Pussy.

Christopher: Hey, I'm not a pussy.

Hector: *(To all of them)* Fucking pussies! *(He tries to move the sink once again. He struggles.)*

*(*Mary *joins him. They struggle together.)*

*(*Joss *looks at* Christopher…*then joins* Hector *and* Mary. *The struggle to move the sink continues.)*

*(*Christopher *watches them struggle, groan, grunt, sweat.)*

(He turns and stares at the audience. He smiles, uncomfortably. Awkward. Not sure of what to do, or say.)

(As the struggle behind him continues…)

Christopher: Hello. *(Beat)* Hello. *(Beat)* How are you? *(Beat)* Welcome. *(Beat…arms wide!)* WELCOME! Thank you for um uh… Thank you for coming. How are you? *(Beat)* Yes. Yes…how are you? *(Smiles… then attempts to "act")* "To be or not to be… that is the question…"

(Smiles…then acts) "Out out brief candle…" *(Smiles… then acts)* "Attention must be paid!" *(Smiles… then acts)* "Friends, Romans, Countrymen…" *(Smiles… then acts)* "Strike, Strike, Strike, Strike!" *(Rips his shirt off)* "STELLAAAAAAA!!!!!!"

(HECTOR, exhausted, gives up the struggle.)

HECTOR: Fuck it, cover it.

MARY: With what?

HECTOR: PUT A FUCKIN COVER ON IT!

(JOSS takes off her apron and puts it over the kitchen sink, like a tablecloth.)

(They all look at the audience. Then speak as though the audience never noticed it was a kitchen sink in the first place. Or notices the fact that they're breathing heavy, drenched in sweat.)

JOSS: What a lovely table.

MARY: Yes indeedy…and such a…a lovely…lovely tablecloth to go with it.

HECTOR: *(To the audience)* Ain't as entertaining now, is it, Chuck?

(MARY slaps HECTOR across the face.)

HECTOR: *(To the audience, with monotone insincerity)* Yes—wow—what a lovely table.

(They walk downstage toward CHRISTOPHER.)

CHRISTOPHER: *(To audience)* Tis nobler to somethin' 'bout slings an' arrows an' sticks an' stones an' broken bones, words an' ever after.

(HECTOR punches CHRISTOPHER in the gut.)

CHRISTOPHER: Ow.

(HECTOR punches CHRISTOPHER again.)

CHRISTOPHER: Ow again.

HECTOR: Straighten up, ya don't feel pain.

CHRISTOPHER: The heck I don't.

MARY: What about this?!

(MARY *kicks* CHRISTOPHER *in the shin.*)

CHRISTOPHER: Triple ow.

(JOSS *kicks him in the shin.*)

CHRISTOPHER: What the hell are you doing?

JOSS: It doesn't hurt, stop lying!

CHRISTOPHER: It hurts, it fucking hurts!

(HECTOR *pulls out a gun and shoots* CHRISTOPHER *in the stomach.*)

HECTOR: You aren't real.

CHRISTOPHER: Oh yeah, tell that to my blood that's bleeding!

(HECTOR *shoots* CHRISTOPHER *in the knee.*)

CHRISTOPHER: OW, STOP IT!

HECTOR: We aren't fucking real!

(HECTOR *shoots* CHRISTOPHER *in both thighs.*
CHRISTOPHER *shoves a knife into* HECTOR's *calf.*)

HECTOR: What the fuck are you doing?

CHRISTOPHER: Oh, I thought we weren't real, asshole!

(HECTOR *shoots* CHRISTOPHER *again—runs out of bullets. He jumps on* CHRISTOPHER *and starts beating him with the butt of his gun...as* CHRISTOPHER *repeatedly stabs and stabs and stabs* HECTOR *in the leg.*)

JOSS: *(English accent)* "The rain in Spain falls mainly on the plain, the rain in Spain falls mainly on the plain, the rain in Spain falls mainly on the plain—"

MARY: Shut the fuck up, bitch!

(MARY *yanks* JOSS's *hair.*)

JOSS: You shut the fuck up!

(They fight and pull each other's hair as they tumble to the ground…)

(…while CHRISTOPHER *begins to stab* HECTOR *in the chest…)*

(…as HECTOR *pounds the gun into the side of* CHRISTOPHER's *head.)*

MARY: No, you—

JOSS: —YOU!—

MARY: —No, YOU!—

JOSS: —YOU!!—

MARY: —No, YOU!—

JOSS: —YOU!!

MARY: —No, YOU!!—

JOSS: —YOU!

HECTOR: Die, motherfucker, DIE!

*(*JOSS *and* MARY *take turns pounding each other's heads into the floor.)*

JOSS: DIE!

MARY: DIE!

CHRISTOPHER: DIE!

HECTOR: FUCKING DIE!

MARY: DIE!

JOSS: DIE!

CHRISTOPHER: DIE!

ALL: *(Together)* DIE! DIE! DIE! DIE! DIE! DIE! DIE! DIE! DIE! DIE!

(They switch: now CHRISTOPHER *and* JOSS *attack each other…)*

(...as HECTOR *and* MARY *attack each other.)*

ALL: *(Together)* DIE! DIE! DIE! DIE! DIE! DIE! DIE!

JOSS: FUCKING DIE YOU MOTHERFUCKER!!!!

ALL: *(Together)* DIE-DIE-DIE-DIE-DIE!!!!

(They're all spent. They collapse. Covered in blood. The floor is covered in blood too. Each of them alone. Apart from one another. Splayed out on the ground. Breathing heavy.)

(For a long time... Almost a full minute.)

(Until, finally...)

HECTOR: I don't feel so good.

JOSS: I feel like crap.

CHRISTOPHER: Why am I feeling? I'm not supposed to feel.

MARY: I'm not supposed to feel either.

CHRISTOPHER: I don't remember anything, why do I feel something?

MARY: I remember my backstory.

HECTOR: Fuck your backstory! I'm fuckin dyin here but I can't die!

JOSS: *(Calm)* I can't sleep. I'm so tired but I can't sleep. I can't dream.

HECTOR: I dream. I have lotsa dreams. I dream I'll... someday... someday... *(Lifts his head, looks toward the audience, stares, beat...)* Someday they'll come true.

(Lifting her head, looking toward the audience:)

JOSS: I can't ever fall asleep. I want...to sleep.

CHRISTOPHER: *(Lifting head toward audience)* "Per chance to dream."

HECTOR: *(To* CHRISTOPHER*)* NO MORE! NO MORE!

MARY: I've never been a ballerina. I've never been given the chance. Not for ballet. *(Looking out toward audience)* Why have I never been given the chance?

HECTOR: A cowboy. I wanna be a cowboy.

JOSS: I'm tired. I'm so so so…tired.

CHRISTOPHER: …Me too.

HECTOR: …Yeah… Me too.

MARY: …Me too.

(They continue staring straight out, directly at the audience.)

(Pause)

(They speak to each other, but never take their eyes off the audience.)

HECTOR: G'night.

(Beat)

MARY: Goodnight.

(Beat)

CHRISTOPHER: Yes. Goodnight.

(They keep their eyes open, staring out. No one sleeps.)

(Pause)

JOSS: Goodnight.

(Silence…as they continue staring out. Straight ahead. Eyes open.)

(They continue to stare out for a long time. As the lights slowly fade to black.)

END OF PLAY

BEAUTY AND LIGHT

BEAUTY AND LIGHT was produced in Collaboraction's Sketchbook 2005 Festival in Chicago, directed by Anthony Moseley.

CHARACTERS & SETTING

JAMAICAN MAN, *early 50s*
GIRL, *9, white*
MOTHER, *30s, white*
FATHER, *40s, white*
MEXICAN WOMAN, *50s*
BLACK TEEN
WHITE TEEN
ASIAN WOMAN, *70s*

Ensemble, diverse and numerous

New York City. Times Square. Subway platform.

for my sister Brigette

(An N Y C subway platform. Times Square station. Rush hour. A JAMAICAN MAN, early 50s, strums an acoustic guitar. He is barefoot. His clothes are tattered and dirty. He is disheveled and unshaven. He sings brokenly—almost in a monotone.)

JAMAICAN MAN:
I see beauty
I see light
I see beauty
I see light
I see beauty
I see light
I see beauty
I see light

(He continues singing as straphangers ignore him, pass by, enter and exit subways, and occasionally throw a few coins in his guitar case.)

JAMAICAN MAN:
I see beauty
I see light
I see beauty
I see light
I see beauty
I see light

(A young white GIRL, 9, walks along the platform with her white MOTHER and FATHER, well-dressed tourists with shopping bags, who argue as they go:)

MOTHER: You'e a LIAR!!!

FATHER: I didn't wanna come ta New York in the first place!!!!

MOTHER: LIIAAARRRR!!!!!!!!!!

FATHER: I wanted ta go to Hawaii!!!!!

MOTHER: But your MOTHER lives HERE!!!!!

(The arguing couple exits. Their daughter stays behind. She approaches the JAMAICAN MAN. *She stops a few feet away. She watches and listens silently. The* JAMAICAN MAN *has been singing throughout:)*

JAMAICAN MAN:
I see beauty
I see light
I see beauty
I see light
I see beauty
I see light

(The young GIRL *joins him…softly:)*

GIRL/JAMAICAN MAN: *(Together)*
I see beauty
I see light
I see beauty
I see light
I see beauty
I see light

(30 seconds, then: A MEXICAN WOMAN, *50s, selling churros—never leaving her small sales table—begins to sing:)*

MEXICAN WOMAN/GIRL/JAMAICAN MAN:
I see beauty
I see light
I see beauty
I see light
I see beauty
I see light

(Two TEENAGED BOYS *come running in—one white, one black. The white teen steals money from the guitar case as he spits on the* JAMAICAN MAN:)

WHITE TEEN: Get a job muthafucker!

BLACK TEEN: Be givin' niggas a bad name, greazy-ass bitch! *(Spits)* He still singin, this muthafucka!

WHITE TEEN: Stop singin' bitch! *(He spits on him again.)*

BLACK TEEN: Whaddaya deaf, muthafucka? Think he R Kelly, some shit.

WHITE TEEN: Thanks for the hat. *(He swipes the hat off the* JAMAICAN MAN*'s head. He puts it on his own head.)*

(The two TEENAGERS *laugh and walk off.)*

(The singing continues—it never stopped—the tone remains unchanged.)

(An elderly ASIAN WOMAN *gently wipes the saliva from the* JAMAICAN MAN*'s face. He very subtly—almost unnoticeably—acknowledges the kind gesture. The* ASIAN WOMAN *throws away the tissue and joins the others in song.)*

ASIAN WOMAN/MEXICAN WOMAN/WHITE GIRL/
JAMAICAN MAN:
I see beauty
I see light
I see beauty
I see light

(Uninterested subway riders continue to pass by. Semi-interested riders slow down as they pass. Others stop and watch and listen. And sing. One after another after another after another after another. The hurry they were once in slowly disappears.)

(Old, young, black, white, Asian, Latino, Middle Eastern, Native American, Wall Street suits, hip-hop jersey-clad youths, homeless, college students, high school kids, blue

collar, police officers, N Y C transit workers, bootlegged C D/D V D sellers, salesmen of counterfeit purses and watches, etc. They all form a semi-circle around the JAMAICAN MAN, *their backs to the audience. Eventually, however, they all slowly turn, facing the audience. The* JAMAICAN MAN *elevated ever-so-slightly above them.)*

ALL:
I see beauty
I see light
I see beauty
I see light
I see beauty
I see light
I see beauty
I see light
I see beauty
I see light

(They continue for a long time.)

(Lights slowly fade to black.)

END OF PLAY

www.ingramcontent.com/pod-product-compliance
Lightning Source LLC
Chambersburg PA
CBHW052139090426
42741CB00009B/2150